D1557889

DIGGING UP
the Past

Machu Picchu

Essential Library
An Imprint of Abdo Publishing | www.abdopublishing.com

Machu Picchu

BY MARY MEINKING

CONTENT CONSULTANT
BETHANY L. TURNER, PHD
DEPARTMENT OF ANTHROPOLOGY
GEORGIA STATE UNIVERSITY

www.abdopublishing.com

Published by Abdo Publishing, a division of ABDO, PO Box 398166, Minneapolis, Minnesota 55439. Copyright © 2015 by Abdo Consulting Group, Inc. International copyrights reserved in all countries. No part of this book may be reproduced in any form without written permission from the publisher. Essential Library™ is a trademark and logo of Abdo Publishing.

Printed in the United States of America, North Mankato, Minnesota
032014
092014

THIS BOOK CONTAINS
RECYCLED MATERIALS

Cover Photo: Kelsey Green/Shutterstock Images
Interior Photos: Kelsey Green/Shutterstock Images, 2; Mark Skalny/Shutterstock Images, 6; Tomaz Kunst/Shutterstock Images, 9; iStockphoto/Thinkstock, 11; Richard Laschon/Shutterstock Images, 11 (inset); Shutterstock Images, 14, 23, 28; North Wind Picture Archives, 18, 66; GDA/AP Images, 21; Thomas Blackshear/National Geographic Image Collection/Glow Images, 25; Hiram Bingham/National Geographic Society/Corbis, 26, 33, 49, 69, 73; H. L. Tucker/National Geographic Society/Corbis, 34; Jarno Gonzalez Zarraonandia/Shutterstock Images, 36; Hiram Bingham/National Geographic Image Collection/Glow Images, 38, 74; Hughes Herv/Hemis.fr/SuperStock, 44; Ralf Broskvar/Shutterstock Images, 46; Bob Child/AP Images, 50; Douglas Healey/AP Images, 54; Bob Krist/Corbis, 56; Yu Lan/Shutterstock Images, 60; Chris Rainier/Corbis, 62; Corbis, 76; Jerome Stubbs/Shutterstock Images, 79; Narongsak Nagadhana/Shutterstock Images, 81; Henry Clay Gipson/Frederic Lewis/Getty Images, 84; Library of Congress, 87; Michele Falzone/JAI/Corbis, 88; Karel Navarro/AP Images, 91; Reuters/Mariana Bazo/Corbis, 93; Joel Shawn/Shutterstock Images, 96

Editor: Arnold Ringstad
Series Designer: Becky Daum

Library of Congress Control Number: 2014932248

Cataloging-in-Publication Data

Meinking, Mary.
 Machu Picchu / Mary Meinking.
   p. cm. -- (Digging up the past)
Includes bibliographical references and index.
ISBN 978-1-62403-234-9
1. Incas--History--Juvenile literature. 2. Incas--Antiquities--Juvenile literature. 3. Machu Picchu Site (Peru)--Juvenile literature. 4. Cuzco Region (Peru)--Antiquities--Juvenile literature.   I. Title.
985--dc23

                                              2014932248

CONTENTS

Mysterious Gem in the Sky

High in the Andes Mountains of South America sits Machu Picchu, a breathtaking granite royal estate built by the Inca people of Peru. Surrounding the city is the site's most recognizable trait, a collection of hundreds of stone terraces. The terraces look like an enormous set of stairways emerging out of the dense jungle below.

Once reserved for royalty and their workers, Machu Picchu is now visited by thousands of tourists each year.

The Inca believed the natural environment around them was sacred. They worshipped the sun, mountains, and rivers. The location where they established Machu Picchu incorporated all of these aspects. The site's developers created structures that looked almost as though they sprouted from the earth.

The city stretched along the narrow ridge between two magnificent mountain peaks, Machu Picchu and Huayna Picchu, which the Inca believed brought them closer to their sun god, Inti. Thousands of feet below the sheer mountainside, the sacred Urubamba River surrounds the estate on three sides.

CROWN JEWEL

Machu Picchu is among the best-known and most popular archaeological sites in the Western Hemisphere. Each year, hundreds of thousands of tourists visit the stone estate, which was built in the 1400s in what is now Peru. Its construction, purpose, and abandonment make it one of the most mysterious and fascinating places on Earth.

This magnificent estate could not have been in a more out-of-the-way place. It is not located on a main road or near a large city. Instead, it sits on a steep ridge in the Andes, approximately 1.5 miles (2.4 km) high.[1] The area is known for landslides and earthquakes, making it an especially challenging

The Temple of the Sun is located near the center of Machu Picchu.

site for Machu Picchu's architects.

The Inca construction workers who built Machu Picchu also faced other hurdles. They had no easy way to cut the tons of granite rock needed to build the city. They also lacked sturdy working animals to move rock from quarries to the building site. Their accomplishment astounds archaeologists still today.

WELCOME TO MACHU PICCHU

Hundreds of magnificent stone buildings dot the landscape of Machu Picchu. The only round building in the city is the Temple of the Sun. The temple was built around a giant boulder protruding from the ground. A groove in the rock helped the Inca predict the winter solstice. They could tell the time of the year based on the angle of the sunlight streaming through the eastern window.

The largest building at Machu Picchu is the *kallanka*, or the Great Hall. It has ten doorways through which local farmers and workers would enter for festivals and ceremonial feasts. Many of the city's important religious buildings are located in the Sacred Plaza. There, several structures are centered on a large square. Key buildings there include the Temple of the Three Windows and the Main Temple. The Temple of the Three Windows is framed by three walls that offer views of the sunrise each morning. The Main Temple was constructed from enormous, polished blocks of granite that have shifted over the years. The blocks are no longer perfectly aligned, but the grandeur of the building is still evident in the rows of niches lining the walls. At the center of the city is its highest point. A platform contains a man-sized stone column US explorers called the Intihuatana, or hitching post of the sun.

The Royal Residence was the luxurious home of the emperor himself. It was built with all the modern conveniences of the day, including running water, a private bath, and built-in mortars for grinding corn in the kitchen.

The remainder of the city is checkered with almost 200 stone-block buildings that were used as homes or for storage. Steep stairways, narrow streets, and stone alleyways run through the city. A series of canals zigzag throughout the city, connecting 16 fountains that provided water for all the residents.

WHERE IS MACHU PICCHU?

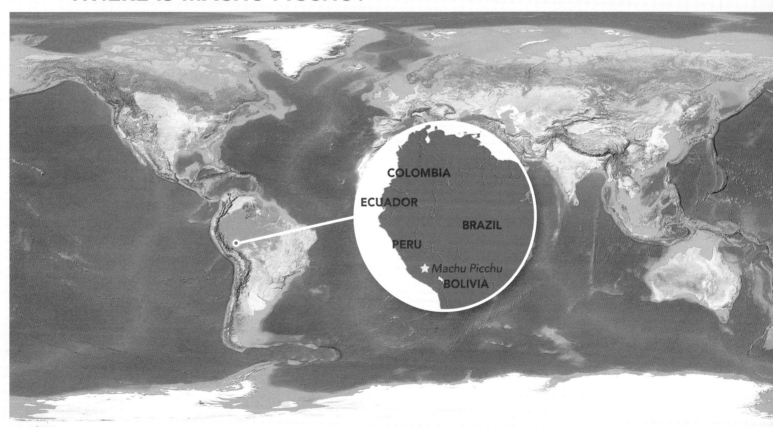

THE OUTSIDE WORLD

The Inca world changed forever when the Spanish conquistadors arrived from Europe in 1532. The invaders stole all the gold and silver they could get their hands on. Although experts believe the Spanish never found Machu Picchu, the site was mysteriously abandoned a few years later. The dense jungle overtook the stone city and its inhabitants vanished. Over the years, archaeologists have suspected European diseases, the Spanish conquest, or a lack of water as possible reasons for the desertion of Machu Picchu.

Nearly 400 years later, in 1911, explorer Hiram Bingham III brought international attention to Machu Picchu when he revealed its existence to the world. He also achieved personal fame. Many Hollywood stories of daring adventurers were modeled after him. In the decades after Bingham discovered Machu Picchu, treasure hunters flocked to the site to hunt for artifacts. International disputes soon raged over the artifacts found at Machu Picchu. Some argued the items belonged to the explorers who found them. Others believed the Inca's descendants should own these key pieces of Inca history.

As Machu Picchu's continued existence and popularity suggest, the Inca site has become an enduring piece of history. It has survived Spanish conquistadors, brutal forces of nature, and millions of tourists. Still, even today, many aspects of this gem of the Andes remain a mystery.

IN THE MOVIES

In 1954, movie actor Charlton Heston starred in the film *Secret of the Incas*, which mirrored Bingham's adventures. Heston's character, Harry Steel, sought an artifact that could magically restore the Inca civilization. Much of the movie was filmed at Machu Picchu, and the filmmakers reportedly employed 500 Peruvians as extras in the film.[3]

Hide and Seek

Hidden high in the Andes for almost four centuries, the ruins of Machu Picchu remained undiscovered by the outside world. The Inca had no written language to record the location of this majestic sanctuary. Only a handful of local people knew of Machu Picchu's breathtaking beauty and could help reveal it to the entire world.

Machu Picchu's remote location kept it from being discovered even in the midst of a Spanish invasion and conquest.

THE INCA

In the early 1400s, the Inca lived in a small kingdom near the city of Cuzco in present-day Peru. Their army defended them against neighboring kingdoms who wanted more land and resources. The more land a kingdom ruled over, the more men they would have for their armies. The Kingdom of Chancas attacked the Inca kingdom in 1438. The elderly King Viracocha Inca decided to flee to a nearby fortress, leaving his son Cusi Yupanqui behind to fight.

Amazingly, Cusi Yupanqui's army won the battle against the invading Chancas. He took over as king and changed his name to Pachacuti, or "earth shaker." The young king was a mighty warrior and led his army to victory against many neighboring kingdoms. The Inca kingdom soon stretched 1,400 miles

INCA RECORD KEEPING

The Inca did not have a written language, so they orally passed on their history and stories from generation to generation. They spoke the Quechua language, which is still spoken in Peru. Although the Inca had no written language, they recorded numbers using a quipu, a complex set of knots on cords. These strings hung from a five-foot (1.5 m) main rope. Inca officials kept records of crops, citizens, and other important numbers on these strings.

(2,300 km) across what are now Bolivia and Peru.[1] He called his new empire Tawantinsuyu, or "the four parts united." Its capital, Cuzco, was located at the intersection of the four kingdoms.

To celebrate his victories and prove his power, Pachacuti ordered the construction of a royal estate in each of the three territories he conquered. These included the twin estates of Pisac and Ollantaytambo, as well as Machu Picchu. Built in approximately 1450, the estates were retreats where the emperor, his family, and other elites could vacation. Pachacuti's successors continued to expand the empire, reaching as far north as modern-day southern Colombia and as far south as southern Chile. At its height in 1532, the empire controlled an estimated 12 million people.[2]

SPANISH CONQUEST

Spanish conquistadors led by Francisco Pizarro invaded the Inca empire in 1532 with one thing in mind: gold. They were drawn by tales of gold to the capital, Cuzco. The 168 conquistadors dominated thousands of

SPANISH INFLUENCE

While in Peru, the Spanish conquistadors took and did what they wanted, and no one could stop them. They took all the precious metal objects they could find and melted them down, even if they had religious or historical significance to the Incas. The Spanish also enslaved the Inca people to work under horrible conditions in silver mines.

The Spanish spread diseases, such as measles, to the Inca, who had never been exposed to such diseases and had no natural defense. Spain ruled over Peru until the nation gained its independence in the 1820s.

local Inca using advanced weaponry, including guns, cannons, and steel swords. The invaders forged alliances with other indigenous groups to assist in the destruction of the Inca Empire. Additionally, the empire had suffered through a ten-year civil war just before the Spanish arrived, weakening it further. The Inca's stone and wooden weapons, though effective in close combat, proved no match for modern long-range armaments. The conquistadors took any precious metals they could get their hands on, including religious items.

Pizarro's conquistadors captured the Inca leader, Emperor Atahualpa, in November 1532 and held him for

Atahualpa's resistance to Christianity and the sovereignty of the Spanish throne contributed to his capture and eventual execution.

ransom. The Spaniards demanded a room filled with gold and two rooms of silver to be paid for his release. Word went out across the entire Inca Empire to gather precious metals to meet the Spanish demands. The Inca people met the Spaniards' demands by May 1533. Still, Pizarro had Atahualpa killed on August 29.

Atahualpa's brother, Manco Capac, was placed on the throne as the new Inca ruler. He soon rebelled against Spanish rule and escaped into a nearby territory in 1536. There, he and the rebel Inca army hid out in the city of Vitcos until the Spaniards tracked them down. Manco Capac again escaped and built a new hidden Inca capital, Vilcabamba, or "plain of the sun." The Inca survived there until the Spanish captured the last Inca ruler in 1572.

The Spaniards remained and ruled over the Inca for hundreds of years, taking all the precious metals they could. Four out of five Inca people died. Some died of diseases brought by the Spaniards. Others died

ABANDONED MOUNTAINTOP

Machu Picchu was used as a royal estate until as late as 1533. Pachacuti's family vacationed there during the winters, even after his death. They went there to relax, entertain, hunt, and worship their sun god. When the Spaniards arrived, the Inca way of life changed throughout the empire. The royal family at Machu Picchu rushed back to Cuzco with their precious metals to ransom Atahualpa's release. Once the royalty left Machu Picchu, the servants, support staff, and craftsmen of Machu Picchu soon abandoned the site too. There was no longer a need for them to cook, grow crops, or perform other tasks around the estate.

of malnutrition as a result of the invaders' looting. Still others died in mines, forced to dig up precious metals for the conquerors.

SPANISH WRITINGS

The Spaniards kept records of their conquest and search for precious metals. However, very little was written about Machu Picchu or other Inca ruins that peppered the Andes. These communities did not have gold, so they remained largely untouched by the conquerors.

In 1565, Spanish diplomat Diego Rodriguez de Figueroa wrote about a place called "Picho" while traveling from Cuzco to Vilcabamba. Historians believe he likely was writing about Machu Picchu. In 1568, another Spanish document mentioned a site called "Picchu or Pijchu." Researchers believe, because of the site's noted location, the name probably referred to Machu Picchu. The document's writer likely got his information from local citizens.

However, there is no evidence Spanish conquistadors actually found or visited Machu Picchu during their time in Peru. The site was not known for its gold stores or its religious, political, or military significance. Even if they had heard of Machu Picchu, uncovering its secrets likely was not a priority.

Spain forbade foreigners from traveling in its territories, including Peru. After the collapse of the Inca Empire, mountain forests grew over Machu

Picchu, and outsiders' memory of the magnificent site faded. For 300 years it became more and more overgrown and was almost lost to history. Still, the locals never forgot its beauty or historical significance.

MAPPING THE WAY

In the 1800s, Spain began allowing foreigners to travel in its Central and South American possessions. In 1865, Italian geographer and explorer Antonio Raimondi published a map of the area along the Urubamba River. On his map was a peak called Machu Picchu, located next to the Urubamba River.

Raimondi is still a popular historical figure in Peru. He is best known for his book *El Peru*, an enormous work that covers a wide swath of Peru's natural history.

TWIN PEAKS

The white granite site of Machu Picchu is nestled between two peaks, Machu Picchu and Huayna Picchu. Its location was chosen because the Inca believed the high altitude made it closer to their sun god.

Machu Picchu is located 45 miles (72 km)—a five-day walk—from the Inca capital of Cuzco. The mountains' names, Machu Picchu and Huayna Picchu, mean "old peak" and "new peak," respectively. The names do not refer to their age but rather to their height, with "old" being the shorter of the two.

Austrian-French explorer Charles Wiener traveled the Urubamba Valley in 1875. In 1880, he published *Perou et Bolivie*, or "Peru and Bolivia." Along with maps, he included local tales about Inca ruins at "still other [ancient Inca] towns, about Huaina-Picchu and about Matcho-Picchu."[3] But when exploring the region, Wiener decided to head downriver to Santa Ana instead of upriver to Machu Picchu, since there was no road and the river was hard to navigate. He made a detailed map of the Urubamba Valley, including two peaks marked "Matchopicchu" and "Huaynapicchu."

In 1904, Peruvian mapmaker Carlos B. Cisneros published *Atlás de Perú*. His atlas included not just maps but also notes about the existence of the ruins of Huayna Picchu. Cisneros wrote, "The entire territory is seeded with ruined Inca populations that offer a great field for investigation by archaeologists, for the numerous objects of precious metal, and the many other things, that surround the shrines and ancient tombs."[4]

Mapmakers created maps of the area for their own personal use or to print and sell for profit. It is not likely any of them ever stepped foot in Machu Picchu, and the location of the ruins probably was based on local rumors.

US INTEREST

In 1909, Harvard University anthropologist William C. Farabee returned to the United States after exploring the lands north of Cuzco. During his travels, he heard a rumor from the locals about a "big city hidden away on the mountain side above the Urubamba Valley."[5] He marked the spot along the Urubamba River on his map.

Around the same time, Albert A. Giesecke was traveling through

The Urubamba Valley is also known as the Sacred Valley of the Inca.

Peru. Originally from Philadelphia, Giesecke was an economist and worked at the University of Cuzco. In January 1911, he went horseback riding through the Urubamba Valley. Locals told him of ruins high up on a nearby mountain, and a guide agreed to take him there. But it was the rainy season, so Giesecke decided to wait for better weather to make the climb.

Soon after learning of the site, Giesecke corresponded with a fellow college professor, Hiram Bingham III. Upon learning what Giesecke had found in the Urubamba Valley, Bingham was anxious to investigate Giesecke's leads and explore the area himself.

Bingham pieced together many clues to the mystery of the hidden site. It was like putting together a giant puzzle. He gathered leads, corresponded with experts, studied maps, and read old Spanish chronicles. Bingham wanted to be the first one to solve the mystery. He needed to put together a great expedition team to help him succeed.

HIRAM BINGHAM

Hiram Bingham III was born in Hawaii to a poor missionary family. He grew up reading adventure novels and wanted to go on adventures himself. As a teen, Bingham traveled to Connecticut to attend Yale University. He married Alfreda Mitchell, the heiress to a jewelry corporation fortune, and he became a professor of Latin American history at Yale.

In 1908, Bingham was a delegate to the Pan-American Scientific Congress, a scientific meeting in Chile. He added a side trip to Peru in 1909 to see Inca ruins. Before long, he took an intense interest in exploration. Bingham led three additional expeditions to Peru's ruins and was credited with discovering Machu Picchu. He later became a US senator.

3

Into the Clouds

Bingham hoped to find a great deal of gold in Peru. So did Yale University, the expedition's sponsor. Bingham put together a seven-man Yale team from diverse academic backgrounds. The team included Bingham, surgeon Dr. William Erving, naturalist Harry Foote, topographer Kai Hendriksen, geographer Isaiah Bowman, climbing expert Herman Tucker, and Bingham's assistant, Paul Baxter Lanius.

The Bingham expedition's impressive team of experts traveled to Peru in search of ruins forgotten by the outside world.

Cuzco, like Machu Picchu itself, is located in the Andes.

The team left on June 8, 1911, heading for South America onboard a steamship. When they arrived, Bingham met with Peruvian president Augusto Leguía. Leguía lined up military escorts to accompany the expedition. The escorts came along not just for protection but also to keep an eye on what the foreign explorers were doing.

While in Peru's capital, Lima, Bingham had more clues to track down. He met with archivist Carlos Romero to review some newly uncovered Inca clues from a 1639 Spanish chronicle. Bingham also purchased locally produced maps of the Urubamba River valley.

The team traveled by ship and train to Cuzco, the ancient Inca capital. Bingham finally met with Albert Giesecke in person after corresponding with him by mail. Giesecke told Bingham to find a farmer named Melchor

Arteaga. Arteaga had told Giesecke of ruins on a mountain, and he could lead Bingham to their location.

BINGHAM'S EXPEDITION

The mission of the expedition was to explore and document the geography, geology, and archaeology of the area. To accomplish this, Bingham divided the expedition into three teams.

The first team, including Bowman and Lanius, was to identify and map the Andes in the surrounding area. The second team, including Hendriksen and Tucker, was to map the valleys and villages along the Urubamba and Vilcabamba Rivers. The third team, including Bingham, Erving, and Foote, was to collect plant and animal samples and to search for Inca ruins. A Peruvian soldier accompanied each team. The teams divided their supplies and departed Cuzco on July 19, 1911.

Following Giesecke's directions, Bingham tracked down Arteaga. The farmer had offered to guide Giesecke to the ruins, and Bingham hoped Arteaga would make him the same offer. Sergeant Carrasco, the Peruvian soldier who accompanied Bingham's group, talked to Arteaga in the local indigenous Quechua language. The men, he said, were "interested in the architectural remains of the Incas, and were looking for the palace of the last Inca." Arteaga said "there are some very good ruins in this vicinity—in fact,

INCA BUILDING BLOCKS

The Inca left behind a great deal of architecture and many building projects. When Pachacuti took over as the Inca ruler in 1438, he embarked on a mission to reshape the Inca world. He began with a major rebuilding campaign. He reorganized the capital city. In Cuzco, old buildings were torn down and new temples and palaces were built in their place. The workers used a new architectural style of stonework. Smooth stones were cut and fit together so precisely that razor blades could not be slid between them. Another building project was the Inca Trail. Thousands of miles of roads built by earlier civilizations were expanded and upgraded into stone-covered highways to move troops and messengers.

some excellent ones on the top of the opposite mountain, called Huayna Picchu and also on a ridge called Machu Picchu."[1] Bingham remembered the names of these places from his research and knew he had to visit them. He hired Arteaga to guide him to the ruins.

MOUNTAIN CLIMBERS

On July 24, Bingham was ready to ascend the peaks of the Andes. But the weather did not cooperate. Low clouds hid the ridge in a cold, rainy mist. Arteaga said it was too slippery to climb. Bingham offered to pay extra if they could make the climb that day anyway. Arteaga agreed, and they started off. Only Bingham and Sergeant Carrasco decided to go on this outing. The others stayed at camp.

The three men cut through the brush until their path was blocked by a waterway. A cobbled-together bridge, made of several long, thin logs tied with vines, spanned the river. Arteaga and Carrasco took off their shoes and walked across the bridge like tightrope walkers. Bingham was not as surefooted, so he got down on his hands and knees and crawled across the rickety bridge.

The men climbed for hours through dense jungles and on steep, slippery slopes. Exhausted, they reached a grass-covered hut where local indigenous farmers welcomed them with gourds of cool water and cooked sweet potatoes.

THE CHILD LEADS THE WAY

Arteaga decided to stay with the farmers instead of taking the men to the ruins. In his place he sent a local farmer's eight-year-old son, Pablito, as their guide.

Bingham wrote, "Hardly had we left the hut and rounded the promontory than we were confronted with an unexpected sight, a great flight of beautifully constructed stone-faced terraces, perhaps a hundred of them."[2]

DIGGING
DEEPER

Photographing the Ruins

Bingham wanted to document the expedition through photographs. He asked George Eastman, founder of the Eastman Kodak camera company, to donate a camera to the expedition. Eastman gave a camera to each member of the expedition. The small, resilient cameras he provided were among the most sophisticated and expensive cameras of their time. The expedition also took along a special panoramic camera and tripod to take landscape photos.

For each shot, the explorers needed to manually wind the film, focus on the subject, set the width of the aperture, and select the shutter speed. Bingham took detailed notes in

his journal of the settings he used for each shot. Because of the limited technology of the time, the photos were not printed on paper until the men returned to Connecticut. In all, the 1911 Yale Peruvian Expedition team took more than 12,000 pictures.[3] The cameras were dependable witnesses to the sites and artifacts the team saw in Peru.

Before the brush covering the site was cleared, it would have been easy to miss the ruins at Machu Picchu.

The terraces were covered in centuries of plant growth. The farmers had cleared off just enough of the area to plant their crops of maize and potatoes.

Bingham and Carrasco continued to follow Pablito along a terrace and into the dense forest. "Suddenly I found myself confronted with the walls of ruined houses built of the finest quality of Inca stone work . . . walls of white granite ashlars [finely cut stones] carefully cut and exquisitely fitted together," Bingham remembered.[4]

Even though the site was covered in dense brush, the boy knew his way through the maze of trees, vines, and thickets. He showed the men a stone-lined cave, which might have been a royal mausoleum, a semicircular building that resembled Cuzco's Temple of the Sun, and a temple lined with niches.

The men marveled at the beauty of the buildings and the fact there was no mortar used in the walls. "There were no ugly spaces between the rocks. They might have grown together," Bingham said.[5] He saw huge boulders in the walls. He estimated they weighed up to 15 short tons (13.6 metric tons) each. For five hours, Bingham measured, took notes, and photographed the site. He took 26 photographs of Machu Picchu's architecture and the landscape. Bingham also sketched a map of the area in his notebook. When the sun began setting, the men returned to camp.

> "It seemed like an unbelievable dream. . . . It fairly took my breath away. What could this place be? Why had no one given us any idea of it?"[6]
>
> —HIRAM BINGHAM

DISCOVERIES UNCOVERED

Bingham found the site was rich in beautifully constructed buildings but poor in retrievable artifacts. Machu Picchu was overgrown with dense vegetation, and looters had already been there.

The Inca likely used the Intihuatana as a sundial.

Still, there were a few unusual built-in artifacts that intrigued Bingham. One was at the highest point of the site. It consisted of a tall column sticking up from a large, carved boulder. Bingham believed each winter solstice priests would pretend to toss a rope around the sun and hook it to the column so it could not move farther north and leave the Inca in darkness. He referred to the artifact as the Intihuatana, or "hitching post of the sun." Bingham's interpretation was never supported by strong evidence.

On one of the temple walls, Bingham found an inscription that disturbed him greatly. It read, "Lizarraga, 1902." The writing suggested at least one person had been to the ruins nearly a decade before Bingham. He hoped it had not been another scholar who could publish an article and claim credit for discovering Machu Picchu.

RETURNING EMPTY-HANDED

Bingham returned to his camp that evening and wrote in his journal. "Fine ruins—much better than Choqq," he wrote, referring to ruins he had visited in 1909.[7] But since Machu Picchu did not have the riches Bingham had hoped to find, he and his men packed up and continued exploring Peru. In December 1911, Bingham presented his archaeological findings to scholars in Lima and left Peru.

On the boat ride home, Bingham decided he needed to return to Peru. He telegraphed ahead to the United States to create a sensation in the press over their expedition. He hoped to capitalize on the excitement to raise funds for another expedition.

Even though he did not find gold or silver, Bingham claimed Machu Picchu's true value lay in its buildings. Bingham said to the press, "We did the next best thing and filled up our notebooks with data and our minds with memories of what we saw."[8]

4

Return to Peru

Bingham returned home an archaeological hero.
Though he did not truly discover Machu Picchu, he
had been the first person to photograph it and make
the site known to the outside world. Still, there was
much more to uncover at the site.

Following the success of his first expedition, Bingham was eager to return
to Peru.

FUNDING THE EXPEDITION

Bingham knew several potential investors, including the National Geographic Society, Yale University, and even President William Howard Taft, a Yale graduate, were interested in funding another Peruvian expedition. The only problem was Peruvian laws prevented removal of antiquities from the country. Bingham wanted to excavate Machu Picchu, but only if he could bring his finds back to the United States.

Bingham and President Taft worked together to bring a collection of Inca artifacts to Yale for study and display in its museum. Taft ordered the US diplomat in Peru

NATIONAL GEOGRAPHIC'S INTEREST

The National Geographic Society began in 1888 as a club for intellectuals and military men of Washington, DC. It soon produced a monthly magazine distributed worldwide. As of 1911, it had never supported an archaeological dig. But the magazine's editor, Gilbert H. Grosvenor, thought archaeology was important to his readers. With all the press surrounding the Yale Peruvian Expedition's return in December 1911, Grosvenor believed the Machu Picchu expedition could be the story the society was waiting for. The April 1913 issue of *National Geographic Magazine* was written by Bingham and devoted entirely to the 1912 expedition to Machu Picchu. It featured 244 photographs from the site.

to work with the Peruvian president, Leguía, to find a compromise. They decided that at the end of the archaeological season, half the treasures found at Machu Picchu would go to Yale and the other half would stay in Peru. No other institution could explore Peru during this time, giving Yale a monopoly over the Peruvian excavations. The Peruvian Congress needed to approve the deal, but the legislative body was on recess. However, Leguía's word was as good as law, so the Yale Peruvian Expedition proceeded. Yale University and the National Geographic Society donated $25,000 (more than $500,000 in today's money) toward the 1912 Yale Peruvian Expedition.[1] Bingham and his team embarked on their journey to Peru on May 16, 1912.

CLEARING THE SITE

The Yale Peruvian Expedition arrived in Machu Picchu in July 1912 and got to work right away. The local governor rounded up 11 farmers and jailed them to prevent them from running away.[2] He handed them over to the expedition when they arrived. Though the locals were paid, they were taken away from the important job of tending their crops. They basically became forced labor for the expedition, and they resented their treatment.

Thick scrub and trees were growing out of Machu Picchu's walls, terraces, and open areas. The crew of locals began clearing three centuries of vegetation growth with axes, machetes, shovels, and crowbars. They set fires to burn off the underbrush on the ridge. Bingham wanted the site to look as though the Incas had departed just days before. He wanted Machu Picchu to look perfect for the photographs he planned to take.

MACHU PICCHU'S STRUCTURES

Once the smoke cleared, the majestic Machu Picchu emerged. With the original stonework exposed, it became obvious how well the Inca worked with the topography of the site to create a balance between nature and the estate's structures. The estate covered more than five square miles (13 sq km).

Most of the buildings and terraces were just as the Incas left them, though their thatched grass roofs had disintegrated and some walls had fallen down over time or from earthquakes. The walls could be repaired, but the explorers had to use their imagination to visualize what the buildings looked like with thatched roofs.

The city was crisscrossed by narrow stairways between the buildings. They varied from three or four steps cut out of a single granite boulder to more than 150 steps carved from individual stone blocks.

HOMES SWEET HOMES

Pachacuti, his family, and elites came to Machu Picchu to entertain dignitaries, participate in religious ceremonies, observe astronomical movements, and relax. There were 14 *kancha*, or compounds, one for each elite family group. The elite's compounds each had a single main entrance with a doorway. The entrance led to a central open patio surrounded by various buildings used for sleeping, cooking, and storage. The buildings had trapezoidal windows, doorways, and niches carved in the walls. All were narrower at the top than the

PRIMITIVE ARCHAEOLOGY

The expedition's collection practices were advertised as archaeology to the press, but their goal of removing material was far from the professionalism of archaeological expeditions of today. All expedition members were given a binder of information written by Bingham. It told the members where to look for artifacts, what to collect, how to collect, and what to record. Under "What to Collect" it noted, "it would be desirable to bring in not only remains of man, bones, sherds, artifacts, etc. but also the bones of any animal found associated with him."[3] Still, Bingham's first excavations were among the most scientific and systematic of their time. Only in his later expeditions did the goal become simple looting.

It was not until the site was
cleared that the explorers
fully understood the scope of
Machu Picchu.

bottom. Many of their walls were covered in yellow clay plaster.

The Royal Residence was the home of Pachacuti and his family when they visited Machu Picchu. His compound was the same size as the other compounds, but it had superior quality stonework. Some walls were covered in stucco made from red clay. The Royal Residence was the first in line to receive water from the spring. It also had a private bath with the only bathtub and private toilet in Machu Picchu.

A total of 150 homes were at Machu Picchu, housing a maximum of 750 residents. The elite had servants, who had their own homes within their compounds or nearby. Other support staff, craftsmen, and farmers serving the city residents lived outside the city's walls.

TEMPLES AND PUBLIC BUILDINGS

Machu Picchu had more buildings used for religious activities than any other Inca estate. There were approximately 30 sacred buildings at Machu Picchu. One building, the Temple of the Sun, stood out from the rest with its curved walls. Inside this *torreon*, or tower, was a sacred rock outcropping in the shape of a puma that took up most of the room. It had a channel cut in the rock. Every year on the winter solstice, light from the eastern window shone directly along the channel. Many rituals and religious sacrifices were held in the Temple of the Sun.

A large public building stood outside the city's walls. It had ten doors through which guests and neighboring farmers could enter for ritual feasts. The *kallanka*, or Great Hall, was perfect for entertaining large groups. Bingham's team found a big pile of potsherds outside it. Most of the broken pottery came from drinking vessels called *qeros*. The Incas drank *chicha*, a ceremonial maize beer, during special events.

5

Widening the Search

Local laborers and US engineer Ellwood C. Erdis began digging in the Sacred Plaza on July 22, 1912. Erdis previously had been a gold miner and worked laying railroad tracks across the Andes, so he was used to hard work. Bingham hoped buried treasure was hidden under the ground. With pickaxes and shovels, the team dug under the rough altar in the Main Temple. All they found was a layer of boulders. They dug under another temple but found nothing. Disappointed at the lack of treasures and bodies,

Several of the site's temples, including the Temple of the Three Windows, are found near the Sacred Plaza.

DEAD BUT NOT FORGOTTEN

The Inca often placed deceased subjects in burial caves instead of in the ground. They filled the entrance to the cave with stones to conceal the opening. The cave protected the body from the weather, wild animals, and grave robbers. The dead were positioned with their knees pulled up under their chin. A shallow hole was dug in the dirt for the body to sit in so it would not fall over. For special occasions, the mummies were retrieved and placed in wall niches in their family's home or the temples. The Incas treated their dead as though they were still alive. They gave them food such as llama or guinea pig meat and drinks such as maize beer. They even entertained the dead and sought their advice.

Bingham decided it was time to expand the search.

BRIBING THE WORKERS

Bingham ordered the team to search the areas around Machu Picchu for artifacts in *machayes*, or burial caves. He put the expedition's osteologist, George Eaton, in charge. Eaton sent three local farmers in search of burial caves since they knew the area the best. Two days in a row, the farmers came back empty-handed. Eaton learned the farmers believed if they dug up the dead, their actions might curse their crops. Bingham offered to pay a bonus "to anyone who would report the whereabouts of a cave containing a skull and who would leave the cave as he found it."[1]

With the offer of money for finding burial caves, the three farmers had a change of heart. They figured if others found the caves, the crops would be cursed anyway, so they may as well be the ones to find the caves and collect the reward. They reported eight burial caves in one day.

BURIAL CAVES

On July 24, 1912, the one-year anniversary of Bingham's original arrival at Machu Picchu, the farmers led Bingham and Eaton to the burial caves. The guides chopped a path with their machetes as they snaked their way through the thick jungle northeast of the ruins. They stopped and pointed at a small wall made of rough stones. The

Burial caves were among the richest sources of artifacts at Machu Picchu.

GEORGE FRANCIS EATON

George Eaton was born in New Haven, Connecticut, the home of Yale University. His father was a professor of botany at Yale. George followed in his father's footsteps, graduating from Yale and becoming a professor there. He specialized in osteology and paleontology, the study of prehistoric life.

Eaton was a curator at Yale's Peabody Museum. In 1912, he joined the expedition to Machu Picchu. Working with a team of local farmers, he excavated human and animal skeletons, which he studied back home at Yale's museum. Once back in the United States, Eaton married a fellow Yale graduate, Julia Hammer. He later became a lieutenant in the US Navy during World War I (1914–1918).

Overseen by Eaton, Yale's collection of artifacts from Machu Picchu was always controversial to the Peruvian government.

archaeologists pulled away the stones to peer into the burial cave. Inside, they came face-to-face with the body of one of the original inhabitants, sitting in an upright position. A few potsherds littered the cave entrance.

Over the next few days, the farmers led the archaeologists to many other caves on the slopes of Machu Picchu. They found several skeletal remains in each cave, along with some pottery. Some skeletons and pots were in mint condition and others were just fragments. But the caves did not contain the gold and silver Bingham had hoped to find. He concluded the Spanish conquistadors must have taken the Inca precious metals at Machu Picchu. On July 29, Bingham left the Machu Picchu site to continue searching for Vitcos and Vilcabamba in the Andes. He left Eaton in charge of the burial cave excavations.

WHO'S BURIED THERE?

Over the next month, Eaton and the farmers excavated a total of 52 caves, uncovering approximately 164 skeletal remains.[2] Eaton claimed approximately four out of five individuals were women. The remainder were infants, or their sex was unknown. However, Eaton did not take into account the fact the average Inca person was much smaller than a modern North American. Due in part to an adaptation to the high altitude, the Inca skeletons were smaller than the North American skeletons he normally studied. The average

SKULLS TELL MORE

The explorers discovered 45 percent of the skulls they found showed "cranial deformation."[4] As infants, Inca bound these individuals' heads to a board or wrapped them with cloth to shape the skull to a point in the back. Different ethnic groups used cranial modification as a fashion statement and to prove their social status.

The Inca were skilled with shaping stone and also used these skills to bore holes in human skulls, a process known as trepanation. They used this technique to control seizures and reduce swelling when there was head trauma. They removed a part of the skull to release the pressure. Archaeologists found several skulls with one or more of these holes at nearby Inca sites, though none were uncovered at Machu Picchu itself. Many of the skulls showed evidence of healing, meaning the patients survived the trepanation procedure.

Inca adult male was 5 feet, 2 inches (157 cm) tall and the females averaged 4 feet, 11 inches (150 cm).[3] As a result, archaeologists eventually discovered Eaton uncovered many fewer female skeletons than he earlier believed.

None of the caves surrounding Machu Picchu contained precious metals or treasures. No royals were buried inside. If the emperor, his family, or another elite person died while in Machu Picchu, the body was carried back to Cuzco for mummification and proper death rites. This meant the remains found around Machu Picchu likely were those of commoners. They probably were servants, laborers, craftsmen, or farmers who served Machu Picchu's elite.

TAKING IT WITH THEM

Eaton theorized the Inca buried the dead with items they believed people needed on their journey to the afterlife. The archaeologists found llama bones, drinks, charcoal, and personal items with the bodies. Each of the bodies was buried with up to six ceramic containers, including plates, cups, cooking pots, serving platters, elaborate bowls, and more. Archaeologists believe these items were owned, used, and repaired during the dead people's lifetimes.

The commoners at Machu Picchu were also buried with everyday items. Archaeologists found personal grooming items such as metal tweezers and mirrors in the caves. Men and women had little body or facial hair, and they plucked whatever hairs they had. Many people wore tweezers around their necks like necklaces. Bronze mirrors might have aided in hair removal or may have been used for starting fires.

LEAVING NO TREASURE

The Inca emperor, his family, and the elite guests at Machu Picchu dressed in the finest clothes and wore gold and silver jewelry. They drank and ate from silver and gold cups and plates. When they abandoned Machu Picchu, the elite took their valuables with them. This left almost no precious metal objects for Bingham and the expedition to uncover.

The Inca woven clothing almost totally disintegrated over the centuries. They lacked buttons, zippers, or snaps to hold their clothing shut. Instead the women used *tupus*, or shawl pins. Higher-status servants were buried with silver or bronze shawl pins holding their clothing closed, compared to others who had bone shawl pins. The Inca buried individuals with jewelry as well. Some people had several stones arranged around their necks. The stones originally were placed on a string necklace. Over the years, the string decayed. Ear piercing was a rite of passage of Inca males. They wore large ear ornaments as a symbol of social status. The elites were known as *orejones*, or "big ears."

Weapons and other tools were buried with the dead. Eaton's crew and later archaeologists found bronze crowbars, stone tools, jewelry, and tools used to produce metal objects. Weapons were buried as well. They found mace heads that looked like large spiked rings. The heads would have been slid onto wooden clubs. A mace could inflict deadly injuries. The expedition brought the skeletons—along with the items buried with them—to the United States for further research by Eaton and future generations of archaeologists.

A royal tunic was among the articles of clothing found at Machu Picchu.

6

Engineering Marvels

More than 550 years ago, Inca engineers faced the challenge of how to build a city on the steep slope of a mountain that received massive amounts of rainfall. To prevent the structures from washing away, they needed to move and distribute the water. They used solid foundations, sophisticated drainage, and high-quality agricultural soil to solve this problem. Ken Wright, a US water engineer, first uncovered these revelations about Machu Picchu in 1994.

Machu Picchu's terraces made it possible to build the large, complex estate on a mountainside.

BIRTHPLACE OF THE POTATO

The pre-Columbian Andeans were the first to cultivate potatoes, which they originally found as a root growing high in the Andes. They discovered the plant was edible and developed it into dozens of varieties. The Inca grew potatoes as a staple food. They dried the potatoes in the sun, creating a freeze-dried potato pulp called *chuño*.

After the Spanish invaded Peru, they took potatoes with them to Europe, where they eventually became an extremely important crop. One variety of potato, known as the white or "Irish Potato," was the main source of food for Ireland. The nation became so reliant upon potatoes that when disease struck the crop, disastrous famines resulted.

STEP UP

Before engineers could build the city, they needed to create a flat surface. The area was known for earthquakes, so the engineers required a stable foundation. They built almost 700 terraces that stepped up the side of the mountain.

The Inca engineers prepared the site by making a deep foundation under the terraces. More than half of the foundation was hidden underground. Engineers built rock retaining walls that leaned inward to create stability. They filled the walls with layers of differently sized rocks. Larger rocks left over from wall construction were used at the bottom. Above these were smaller rocks, and above the smaller rocks was sandy gravel. At the top was a layer of rich topsoil.

By building the foundation in layers, rainwater and underground water could efficiently drain through the terrace rock. The water passed through each layer and was safely carried away, creating a stable environment for buildings and agriculture.

The terraces were not just used to support buildings. More than 12 acres (4.9 ha) of their area were used for agriculture.[1] Machu Picchu's staff farmers grew maize and potatoes on the terraces. However, the food grown here was unable to fully sustain the entire population of Machu Picchu when the city was at maximum capacity. Produce from neighboring farms was brought in to satisfy the demand, especially when the rulers were in residence, swelling the population.

Inca engineers also developed a way to remove runoff water from the city's thatched roofs and flat surfaces. Machu Picchu's approximately 172 buildings covered 21 acres (8.5 ha), generating a great deal of runoff.[2] A drainage system channeled water through 130 small outlets cut into rock surfaces throughout the city. The system prevented flooded homes, streets, and temples. It also kept the city from sliding down the mountain, helping Machu Picchu last for centuries.

WATER WORKS

The location for Machu Picchu was chosen not only because its builders believed it was close to the sun god, but also because a nearby spring could provide fresh water. The residents required a source of clean water for drinking, bathing, and ritual purposes.

The engineers located a natural spring high above the city. They needed to collect the water and channel it into the city. They carved tightly fitting stones and lined a canal system with them. The canals averaged five inches (12.7 cm) wide by five inches (12.7 cm) deep and could carry 80 gallons (300 L) of water a

Machu Picchu's canal system not only provided water to the estate, but also protected the hillside from erosion.

minute into the city, depending on the season.[3] Gravity pushed the water 2,457 feet (749 m) from its source to the city center.[4]

There were two control points along the canal route where excess water could spill out onto the agricultural terraces or into Machu Picchu's drain before it reached the city's fountains. This way, a day of heavy flowing water or a downpour would not cause the canals or fountains to overflow. Extra water at the end of the line simply flowed into the rain forest below Machu Picchu.

FOUNTAINS

The Inca accessed water in Machu Picchu through a series of 16 fountains. A long stairway known as the Stairway of Fountains paralleled the fountains down the steep slope.

The builders determined where to place the ruler's residence by the location of the spring. His living quarters were the water's first stop along its way to the city. This gave the emperor access to the purest water

WATER SHORTAGE

One theory why Machu Picchu was abandoned was the city ran out of water. However, this is a myth. There was more than enough fresh spring water to support the population of Machu Picchu during the 90 years it was actively used. Data collected by scientists suggests the precipitation in the last decade before the city was abandoned was greater than during any other decade of its occupation.

before it flowed downhill through the residential zone. Pachacuti also had an elaborately carved fountain with a stone enclosure built into his home so he could bathe in privacy for ceremonial rituals. The dirty water passed through a separate drain rather than returning to the water supply.

Each fountain had a stone spout carved at the top to concentrate the jet of water into a rectangular, shallow basin. The resident staff placed their clay water jugs, called *aryballos*, under the jet of water to fill them. Common people collected their water from the fountains and took it home for cooking, drinking, and bathing. Excess water flowed out through a circular drain and on to the next fountain. The last fountain in the line was at the Temple of the Condor. At the temple, the priest used the water for ritual bathing. The remaining water flowed into the rain forest on its way down the mountain.

Machu Picchu's sophisticated water system provided clean drinking water to royals, servants, and guests alike.

WATER JUGS

At least 150 *aryballos* were found at Machu Picchu. These long-necked jugs had two handles. The Inca strung the handles with a rope so people could carry the jugs on their backs. The jugs had a pointed bottom so they would stay upright when set into holes in the dirt.

Jugs were also used to ferment, store, and transport maize beer for large public festivals and rituals. More than 28 percent of the containers found at Machu Picchu were *aryballos*.[5]

STONE WALLS

The Inca took great care in their building process. Sturdy stone walls are one example of their dedication to a lasting city. A typical wall was 2.6 feet (0.8 m) thick at ground level, but some, such as retaining walls, were thicker. The walls got narrower toward the top. The Inca stacked the stones with offset vertical joints, like a brick wall, so they were not stacked right on top of each other. This made for a more stable wall. Rather than using mortar to hold the stones together, Inca engineers created indentations in the stones. This allowed the stones to lock together in a nesting manner.

The Inca engineers designed at least 18 different types of stone

MOVING BIG STONES

The stones used for building Machu Picchu came from numerous surrounding quarries. The main source was Caos Granitico, located south of the Temple of the Three Windows. Some of the largest granite stones weighed up to 14 short tons (13 metric tons) and were up to nine feet (3 m) long.[6]

Since the Inca did not have wheeled carts or draft animals to move large stones, Inca engineers relied upon other techniques to move the stones into position. They placed logs under the rocks, then pushed poles in unison to move the giant rocks along the ground. Laborers used temporary slide-like earthen ramps as inclined planes to move the large rocks uphill. Once the rocks were in position, the Inca removed the ramps.

work for the walls of Machu Picchu. Agricultural terraces featured rough stone walls, while smooth, carved, rectangular stones adorned the emperor's residence.

Modern-day engineers, such as Ken Wright, have compared the methods used at Machu Picchu to construction in cities today. Today's engineers concluded their ancient counterparts planned out every aspect of the city so it would last for centuries to come.

The various types of stone walls were designed for different purposes.

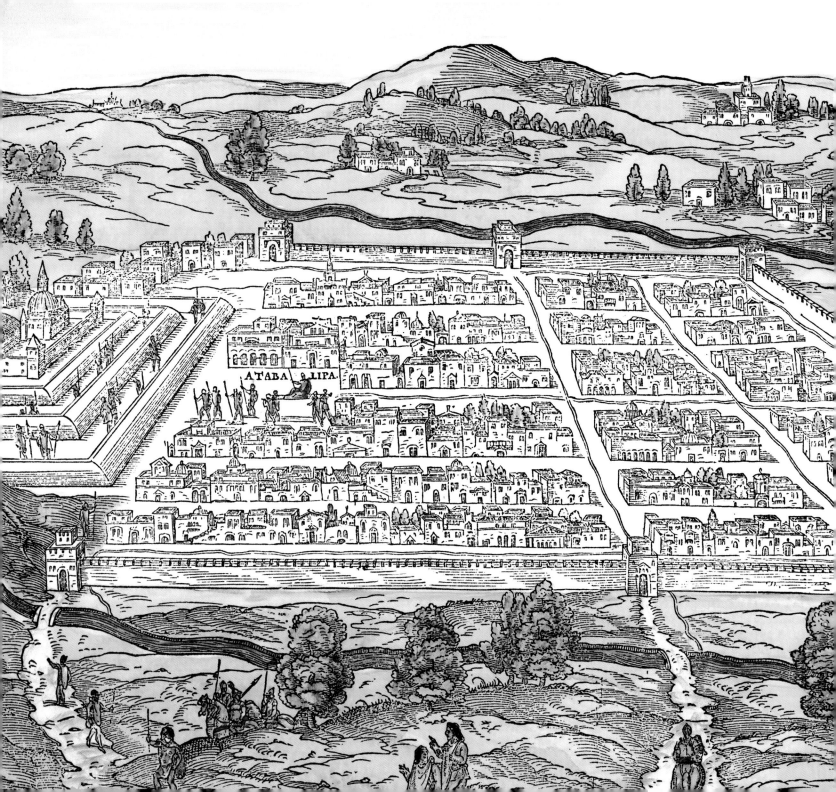

Inca Antiquities

Through his studies of skeletal remains, Eaton discovered an ethnically diverse group of people lived and died at Machu Picchu. There were a few people buried there from the local Cuzco area, but the most common ethnic group came from hundreds of miles away in the Lake Titicaca area. Others came from the north and central coasts and the northern mountain areas.

The city of Cuzco was just one of many sources of Machu Picchu's workforce.

Servants from all over the empire came to Machu Picchu to work for the royal family. Some were people captured during battles in faraway lands. Others worked for the empire's elites and came with their employers from Cuzco. The emperor brought the empire's top craftsmen, masons, and engineers to design and build the city.

The diverse ethnic backgrounds were evident from the food containers found at Machu Picchu. The craftsmen made the containers from different clays and decorated them with the designs and styles of their homeland.

CRAFTSMEN

Eaton and modern-day archaeologists discovered craftsmen of all types lived and worked in Machu Picchu, including metalworkers, stoneworkers, and weavers. Some craftsmen made items for everyday use by the emperor and the elites. Others made items as souvenirs for dignitaries or gifts for foreign nations' rulers. And some of the items the craftsmen made were for personal use.

Not every Inca site had a foundry to produce metal, but Machu Picchu did. Fragments of tin bronze prove metal was produced there. A silver-copper alloy found at the site provides additional evidence the Inca accomplished complex metalwork at Machu Picchu. Craftsmen made bronze crowbars and masonry tools. A ritual knife with a llama head, called a *tumi*,

A wide assortment of pottery was found at Machu Picchu.

showed the people of Machu Picchu experimented with metal casting as well. Archaeologists found hinged metal tweezers at the site. The Inca made the tweezers by hammering cut sheet metal.

The Inca made fabric at Machu Picchu as well. Women spun wool or cotton thread and wove the fabric for clothing and wall art. They used bone weaving tools, called *wichunas*, to pack the threads together.

Stoneworkers made ritual objects, such as jewelry. Many kinds of stone were used. Soft green rock was cut, shaped into small items, then ground and polished. Archaeologists uncovered many pendants for necklaces, small animal miniatures, and good luck amulets at Machu Picchu.

CASH PRIZES

In 1912, Eaton and the farmers found 52 burial caves between July and late August. However, Eaton had to leave the site to visit ruins south of Cuzco. So Ellwood Erdis, the North American engineer, was put in charge of the search for artifacts at Machu Picchu.

He organized the remaining laborers and set rewards for different discoveries. He paid the laborers 80 cents for an entire skeleton, 20 cents for a skull, 20 cents for a whole pot, and 20 cents for a bronze item.[1] The laborers searched high and low in buildings and caves for artifacts.

They found an additional 54 burial caves with mummified

A GIANT ROCK AND A PET DOG

A 60-foot-(18 m) tall rock jutted out of the Machu Picchu slope. Under it, Eaton and the three local farmers discovered a ceremonial terrace, which they called the Rock-Sheltered Terrace. They excavated under the floor of the terrace and discovered the remains of a teenage boy and a man. They also found pottery, a roof-framing stone, llama bones, and charcoal. Eaton wrote about the items his team uncovered. They also found, he said, "the skeleton of a delicately formed woman. . . [with her] personal belongings, her pottery, and the skeleton of her dog. This animal was of a type similar to the Peruvian collie-like Inca dogs."[2] They believed the woman was the high sun priestess and she was buried with her pet dog in the terrace. She must have been a high-ranking person to be buried in such a lovely location with her four-legged companion. The Inca likely thought highly of her.

remains, bringing the total number of discovered caves to 107. The laborers also found complete items or potsherds from 1,650 ceramic containers and approximately 200 metal items. They found bronze, silver, and tin items, but they did not find any gold.

Two unique metal objects stood out from the large collection of artifacts. Erdis wrote in his journal about one item he found in the corner of a room. He found a "bronze knife, with handle decorated with [a] figure of man with breech cloth, on stomach, feet in air, pulling on a rope, to which is attached a fish."[3] He found the other unique piece in a cave. It was a small bronze pin with a tiny hummingbird on top. It still had a piece of string threaded through its hole.

UNUSUAL FINDS

Archaeologists found a few small lime-holding pottery receptacles at Machu Picchu. The Inca added a tiny spoonful of ground limestone to the coca leaves they chewed for medicinal purposes. Coca was bitter, so they added the lime to sweeten it and increase its stimulating effects. The Inca hung the small containers by a cord from their neck or waist.

Archaeologists also found musical instruments at Machu Picchu. They found a ceramic whistle, called an ocarina, near the main gate to the city. Its purpose is unknown, but the shrill sound it makes when blown led some archaeologists to believe the Inca might have used it as a warning alarm if the gate was attacked. A bone flute, called a *quena*, was also found. It was carved from a llama or alpaca leg bone. The instrument had four finger holes on the top and one thumbhole on the bottom.

THE DEBATE

While the men excavated at Machu Picchu, the Peruvian government was changing. President Leguía, who supported the Yale Peruvian Expedition, was not reelected. Political views over the ownership of Inca artifacts were beginning to change.

A month and a half of political debate began over the ownership of Peru's indigenous past. Some in Peru's government believed none of the artifacts uncovered by the Yale group should leave Peru at all. The debate went international as archaeologists from Harvard University in the United States, the British Museum in the United Kingdom, and Berlin, Germany, became involved. Bingham made a public statement suggesting Yale was Peru's archaeological godfather and Peruvians did not care about their indigenous past. This slip of the tongue by Bingham felt like an insult to the Peruvians. They were already skeptical of the archaeologist. The Peruvians had long been exploited by outsiders, first by colonial powers and later by archaeologists who smuggled artifacts out of their country. They wanted to put this cycle to a stop. In the end, Peru's President Guillermo Billinghurst made a deal with the expedition. Bingham wrote a letter to Yale's president explaining the bargain: "[The deal] is to give us full permission to export everything we excavated before the first of December [1912]."[4]

By October 19, 1912, the excavation came to an end. The team packed the bones and artifacts in 93 wooden crates and shipped them via mule train to Cuzco. One month later, the finalized agreement arrived from President Billinghurst. He had made one addition. The artifacts could still leave Peru, but Peru reserved "the right to exact from the University of Yale . . . the return of the unique and duplicate objects it has extracted."[5] The artifacts of Machu Picchu still officially belonged to Peru. When Peru wanted them back, Yale was required to return them.

Bingham's second expedition to Machu Picchu brought back huge quantities of artifacts to the United States.

8

A New Expedition

Bad luck followed Bingham and his expedition on the journey home. They took one ship back to the United States and their artifacts took another. On Christmas Day 1912, the ship carrying the Machu Picchu collection ran aground on Brigantine Shoals, New Jersey. Quick action on the part of the crew saved the precious cargo.

The pages of *National Geographic Magazine* were soon filled with photos from Bingham's expedition.

Word of Bingham's return with the collection of artifacts from Machu Picchu fueled interest worldwide. Bingham spent the spring writing his promised article on Machu Picchu for *National Geographic Magazine*. The editor, Gilbert Grosvenor, liked it so much he made the entire issue about Machu Picchu. The April 1913 issue was titled "In the Wonderland of Peru" and featured Bingham's photos. Grosvenor said Bingham's discovery was "the most important made in South America since the discovery of America."[1] Bingham did not disclose the details of the agreement made with President Billinghurst.

BACK TO PERU

The National Geographic Society was anxious for Bingham's return to Peru. Now that the word was out, the society believed it was in a race with archaeologists from around the world to uncover the pre-Columbian history of the Americas. "Somebody is going to solve the mystery connected with these ancient peoples. Let us get there first," Grosvenor wrote.[2]

The National Geographic Society put $20,000 (nearly $450,000 in today's money) toward a two-year expedition to Peru. Bingham divided his team into two waves. Erdis would lead the first group of the 1914–1915 Yale Peruvian Expedition. His six-man crew left on April 18, 1914, to do reconnaissance work and map the ruins of the region. Bingham planned to join them the following year, setting up an archaeological center near Cuzco where Peruvian and US archaeologists could work together.

More upheaval in the government of Peru proved beneficial to the expedition. The president of Peru, Billinghurst, was overthrown. The new conservative leadership approved the expedition's return. However, there was no guarantee this government would be in place at the expedition's end two years later.

SMUGGLING BUSINESS

While the expedition explored Peru's geography, Bingham began buying a collection of South American antiquities he planned to smuggle into the United States. Bingham wrote to a Cuzco antiquarian, Tomás Alvistur, who offered to sell his collection. Bingham visited Alvistur's museum in 1912 and knew about his impressive finds. Alvistur had collected 366 pre-Columbian artifacts from Inca ruins. Bingham was especially interested in four massive Inca jugs, a green-black stone chalice, a carved stone alpaca and bird, and a beautiful jug originally taken from Machu Picchu by Lizarraga. Lizarraga turned out to be a local muleteer who found some artifacts when he visited the site in 1902.

Bingham struck a deal with Alvistur. He agreed to pay Alvistur money he had received from his wife's family. In return, Alvistur paid off the Peruvian customs officials so Bingham could sneak the artifacts out of Peru. The plan was risky and illegal, but it worked. In mid-September 1914, seven large crates full of artifacts arrived in New York.

BIG SECRET

The unusual artifacts smuggled out of Peru in 1914 could not be documented or publically displayed. All the beautiful pottery and carvings purchased from Alvistur's collection had to remain a secret. The expedition leaders knew officials in Peru could not find out about these smuggled items.

Bingham's group mapped the peaks near Machu Picchu and expanded their hunt for artifacts.

MAPPING AND COLLECTING

The first team arrived in Cuzco on May 19, 1914, and went straight to work. Topographers started mapping the high peaks around Cuzco. Expedition member Osgood Hardy lived with the locals and started learning Quechua, the primary language of the Inca and still the dominant native language in Peru. As directed by Bingham, the team was on the lookout for artifacts for sale. They managed to purchase a few, including a broken pot with a twisted face and a monkey on it.

In mid-May, the expedition's muleteer, Ricardo Charaja, stumbled upon an interesting find. On a 15,600-foot (4,750 m) hill he found a wooden club, a carved wooden boat, and a broken silver sun. The rest of the group helped find the other part of the silver sun, several bronze discs, a bronze breastplate, and a 0.75-inch (1.9 cm) gold circle.[3] Finally, the expedition had found gold in Peru. Erdis made an effort to avoid letting the Peruvians know about the gold they had found.

The items the expedition found may have tumbled down the mountain from where they were placed on the glacier above. The site's name was Inca Churisca, or "frozen Inca." It is believed Inca women and children, chosen for their beauty, were dressed in their finest clothing and then sacrificed along with precious offerings to the mountain in a ritual known as the *capacocha*.

In September, the expedition's surgeon, Dr. Edwin Meserve, decided to leave early. World War I had broken out, and he wanted to enlist in the military to help the United Kingdom. Erdis put gold and other artifacts in the surgeon's personal trunk. It was not searched by the Peruvians, and it left the country. However, Meserve's ship sank, along with the smuggled artifacts. The trunk was recovered in October, and the artifacts were sent to Yale. In November, the expedition's topographer returned to Yale with two-and-a-half skulls, a mummy, and pottery hidden in his steel trunk.

Ollantaytambo shared many features with Machu Picchu, including its terraced construction.

HOUSE OF THE YANKEES

Bingham arrived in Peru in April 1915. He made his way to the expedition's new home base. As part of the 1914 agreement with the Peruvian government, Hardy rented a house in Ollanta, the local town at the foot of another Inca royal estate called Ollantaytambo. There he set up workrooms, a dormitory, bathrooms, a kitchen, a dining facility, a storeroom, and a darkroom. This became Yale's Archaeological Institution, nicknamed *Yanquihausi*, or the "House of the Yankees."

The institution was open to all foreign expeditions in Peru and served as a place where Peruvians and visitors could exchange ideas and collaborate.

But any artifacts found in Peru needed to stay there or at the National Museum in Lima. This new agreement was a small victory for Peru. It was able to keep artifacts and skeletons found by foreign explorers without the expensive task of uncovering them.

MUMMIES ON FIRE

The natives discovered another cave at Machu Picchu filled with mummies, but the cave also had vampire bats. In order to remove the bats, the natives took off some of the mummies' wrappings and set them on fire. When Bingham arrived, he was horrified. He tied a bandana around his face and crawled inside the cave to save what he could. Twenty skulls and a dozen mummies were recovered, but they were charred from the fire.[4]

CITY ON THE HILL

Erdis and six laborers excavated Patallacta, also known as the "city on the hill." They believed the terraces there were the agricultural site that grew additional food for the Machu Picchu residents and elites.

The expedition uncovered a cache of human remains. In one cave, Erdis pulled out 200 skulls and at least a dozen mummies. One was still wrapped in brown and blue cloth, with its hands on its face.

On May 6, Bingham, Hardy, Charaja, and their native guides hacked their way through the forest to find the old Inca Trail, which was paved in smooth stones. They followed the trail up the notch between two summits known as the Warmiwañusca, or "Dead Woman's Pass."

Over the next four days, the team passed waterfalls, lakes, canyons, and the ruins of several ancient villages. On May 13, they reached Machu Picchu, becoming the first foreigners to complete the famous Inca Trail. Upon reaching the city, Bingham said he "nearly wept to see how it had gone back to jungle and brush."[5] It had been only two-and-a-half years, and the jungle was already reclaiming Machu Picchu.

ILLEGAL EXCAVATIONS

Rumors flew throughout Peru that the Yale Peruvian Expedition was illegally excavating and smuggling artifacts out of the country. Some of the wild rumors being circulated indicated the Americans were using earthmoving equipment from the construction of the Panama Canal to excavate archaeological sites in Peru. Other rumors suggested the expedition smuggled out 200 crates of gold artifacts. Some said the Americans brought mummies to life to side with Peru's enemy Chile in an attack on Peru.

Luis Valcárcel, the founder of Cuzco's Historical Institute, and three other members of the institute set off on June 10 to see for themselves what Bingham's group was doing at Machu Picchu. They interviewed native Peruvians along the way and heard the rumors about the Yale group. On June 14, Valcárcel's group saw for themselves how the expedition was behaving at the site. Though the wildest rumors were unfounded, the

members of the Peruvian expedition had been brutal to the ruins. They had removed 200 skulls, torn down walls covered in vines, left giant holes unfilled, and excavated on a massive scale without supervision. It looked more like a brutal treasure hunt instead of a scientific excavation, with total disregard for the site and the human remains. "They've excavated so as not to leave a single potsherd," Valcárcel wrote.[6]

COURT CASE

On June 15, a Cuzco soldier notified Bingham unauthorized excavations were forbidden, and he was barred from exporting artifacts of any kind. After speaking with Erdis, Bingham realized they had excavated without a permit. Seeking a permit in 1914, Erdis had visited all the government agencies he needed to, except one—the Ministry of Justice and Education.

Bingham refused to show the Cuzco soldier the expedition's boxes of artifacts. But Valcárcel's investigators found four artifact-filled boxes the expedition left with a local farmer. They confiscated the boxes as evidence. A hearing was scheduled to determine whether any artifacts had been illegally taken.

In only a few expeditions, an enormous amount of Machu Picchu's history was removed.

Bingham and the members of the expedition knew they were wrong in smuggling artifacts out of Peru. But they hoped they would not get caught. Per the latest law, the 1914–1915 expedition was not to export any artifacts or human remains out of the country.

The hearing began on July 1 with the opening of two of Yale's crates of artifacts. They contained potsherds and an assortment of bones but no gold or silver. A third box labeled "Specials" held a single unbroken pot, a bronze tool, and a bone shawl pin. Bingham appealed to the jury, saying the pot would not even be worth fifty cents in Cuzco.

In the end, the Peruvian government could only prove the Yale Peruvian Expedition was excavating without a license. The authorities were unable to prove the expedition had found gold or silver, bought Inca artifacts, or smuggled items out of the country. The expedition succeeded in removing a vast assortment of archaeological wealth from Peru.

FAREWELL TO PERU

On July 3, Bingham traveled to his team at Ollantaytambo and told them to halt excavations. He made one last trip to Machu Picchu to say good-bye. Then he traveled through the Andes and returned to Lima to negotiate his departure. By the end of August he was on a ship heading back to the United States empty-handed.

Only a few years after his Machu Picchu expeditions, Bingham served during World War I in France.

Erdis was still in Peru trying to extract some of the 74 boxes filled with two short tons (1.8 metric tons) of artifacts from Patallacta. After much debate, Erdis threatened to shame Peru on the international stage in *National Geographic Magazine* by describing how the country was not being cooperative. Peru relented and allowed the entire collection to go to Yale, with the stipulation it be returned to Peru in 18 months. Erdis left Peru on February 3, 1916. The artifacts followed on a separate ship.

9

The Modern Machu Picchu

Beginning in 1911, Peruvians were anxious to protect their cultural history from looters. They passed laws forbidding the removal of artifacts from their country. The debate went on over who owned and could interpret the indigenous artifacts of Peru. Bingham and Yale believed they had education and technology on their side to study the artifacts uncovered at Machu Picchu, and they argued Peru did not have the same tools available.

A road now makes accessing Machu Picchu relatively easy.

BINGHAM'S LATER LIFE

Bingham was elected governor of Connecticut in 1924. He then resigned to fill a vacant spot in the US Senate. He published books on South America and Machu Picchu in the 1920s, 1930s, and 1940s. Bingham was invited back to Peru in 1948 to help inaugurate the opening of a paved road to Machu Picchu. The road was named *Carretera Hiram Bingham*, or the "Hiram Bingham Highway," and it zigzagged up the mountain in a series of switchbacks. It went from the railroad station on the valley floor to the ruins.

Peru's government believed their nation had been stripped of its treasures and the remains of its ancestors. This belief stemmed from the agreement Bingham signed in 1912 in order to have the artifacts loaned to Yale in the first place. It stated Peru could have its artifacts back whenever it wanted them. Peru made its first request for the artifacts in October 1920. Still, the artifacts sat in museums at Yale. For decades, Peru continued requesting the return of its artifacts. Finally, in December 2008, Peru sued Yale in a US federal court for the return of all of the artifacts and human remains taken by the 1912 expedition.

The Peruvian president, Alan García, led protests in the streets of Lima demanding the collection be sent back to Peru. He even asked US president Barack Obama for help. Peruvian officials traveled to the Vatican and requested Pope Benedict XVI's help to resolve the standoff. Yale president Richard Levin sent a delegation to Lima to discuss the matter. The two sides eventually signed a memorandum of understanding. Yale initially requested the right to hold the artifacts for another 99 years, but the request was quickly denied.

In March 2011, the first shipment was sent back to Peru. The second followed in December. Finally, on November 12, 2012, the third and final 127-box shipment of Machu Picchu artifacts was sent back to Peru. This ended the century-long dispute between Peru and Yale University. The artifacts are currently on display at the Casa Concho Museum in Cuzco, Peru.

NEW FINDS AND REEVALUATIONS

Several new artifacts have been found in and around Machu Picchu since Bingham's days at the site. In 1995, Peruvian archaeologist Elva Torres found a 16-carat gold cuff bracelet. This rectangular curved bracelet was approximately 2.35 by 6 inches (8.3 by 15.2 cm) and made from a hammered sheet of gold.

Peruvian president Alan García was present to receive the first shipment of artifacts from Yale.

DIGGING DEEPER

Studying Bones

Tulane University scientist John Verano discovered a great deal about Machu Picchu's inhabitants by studying their bones. Looking at damage, disease, and chemical makeup can hint at the kind of people the bones once belonged to.

For instance, the lack of traumatic injuries to the bones suggests the people were not soldiers. At the same time, they were likely not royals, since they were not buried with luxury items. The absence of arthritis shows the people did not likely engage in difficult physical labor. However, Verano noticed the teeth had many cavities and other issues. The decay can be linked to the high amount of damaging carbohydrates, such as corn, in the upper-class Inca diet.

Studying the chemical makeup of the bones provided more evidence about the people's diets. To measure this, scientists vaporize a small piece of bone and examine it for chemical traces. In the case of the Machu Picchu bones, Verano discovered an unusually high amount of carbon-13 isotopes—a signature of a corn-heavy diet.

The people were clearly not elites themselves. However, they were not subjected to war or difficult agricultural work, and they ate the corn normally associated with elites. Verano concluded the bones likely belonged to the elites' domestic servants.

Studying the bones of Machu Picchu's people reveals a remarkable number of details about their lifestyles.

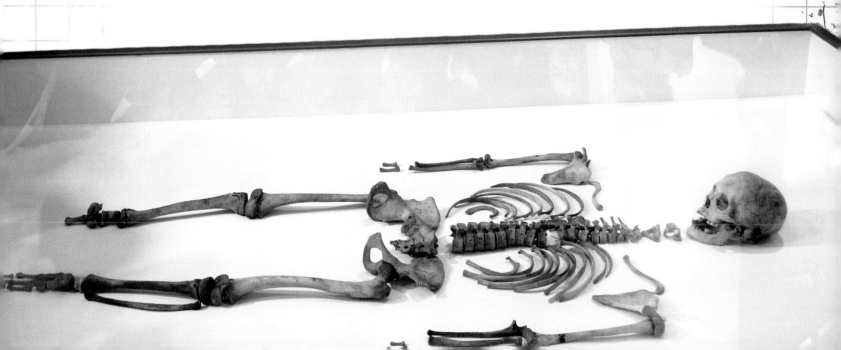

The cuff fit around the forearm of a priest or elite person. It was found among chipped stone rubble beside an underground wall. It likely was placed there as a ritual offering. The archaeologist sent the bracelet to the Cusco Regional Museum.

In 2003, Tulane University professor John Verano reevaluated the human bones excavated in 1912. When Eaton studied the remains back in the early 1900s, he believed the majority of the population at Machu Picchu was female, with four females for every male. Verano examined features of the pelvises and skulls to determine the sex of the adult skeletons. He estimated the ratio was actually 1.5 females for every male.[1]

PRESERVING THE PAST

On January 8, 1981, the Peruvian government named Machu Picchu a Peruvian Historical Sanctuary. The 126 square mile (325.92 sq km) area surrounding Machu Picchu, including its plants and animals, is considered a sanctuary along with the ruins. Peru is trying to conserve the geologic formations and the beautiful surrounding landscape.

In 1983, the United Nations Educational, Scientific, and Cultural Organization (UNESCO) listed Machu Picchu as a World Heritage Site. The listing helped raise awareness about preserving Inca history. It also raised the level of the protection given to Machu Picchu, known as one of the most beautiful World Heritage Sites.

In 2000, 2008, and 2010, Machu Picchu was on the World Monument Fund's Watch List. Its stone structures and agricultural terraces have taken a beating from years of weather fluctuations, wars, earthquakes, and the millions of tourists who visit annually. The steady flow of tourists to Machu Picchu has prompted development and urbanization nearby. In recent years, a luxury lodge was built just steps away from the ruins so visitors can stay close to the site, like the Inca workers did centuries ago. Peru faces a balancing act between meeting the public's desire to visit the site and preserving this cultural icon.

PROTECTING MACHU PICCHU

In 2012, a team of experts from UNESCO visited Machu Picchu to evaluate how well the site was being preserved. Their conclusion was troubling. They called on the Peruvian government to take "emergency measures" to ensure new tourism development projects did not damage Machu Picchu. The nearest town to the site, Aguas Calientes, was growing rapidly as a result of new development projects, and the experts felt the authorities were not taking steps to ensure the protection of Machu Picchu during this growth. Though Peru possesses many archaeological sites, approximately 90 percent of its tourism revenue comes from Machu Picchu.[2]

SHEDDING LIGHT ON THE PAST

Some early archaeologists thought of the Inca as backward because they lacked a written language, the wheel, and steel tools. However, the Inca made technological advances in other areas. They performed brain surgeries, predicted annual solstices, built thousands of miles of paved roads, and developed aqueducts to move water where they needed it to go.

The Inca at Machu Picchu created one of the most recognizable archaeological landscapes in the world, in one of the most challenging natural landscapes of the world—the Andes mountain range. Inca engineers designed the sacred site to perch on a steep slope. Workers moved tons of white granite stone up the mountainside and fit it together with precision.

Even though artifacts and human remains were uncovered there, the real treasure found at Machu Picchu was the site itself. It proved the Inca were master architects, engineers, and stonemasons. By creating a balance between their environment and their artificial structures, the builders of Machu Picchu left us with one of mankind's most incredible archaeological wonders.

People are working to ensure Machu Picchu, among the most impressive remnants of Inca culture, remains both safe and accessible for future generations.

TIMELINE

1438

The ninth Inca ruler, Pachacuti, becomes leader of the Inca Empire after defeating the Chancas.

CA. 1450

The Inca build Machu Picchu as a royal retreat for Pachacuti.

CA. 1533

The Inca abandon Machu Picchu.

1865

Antonio Raimondi publishes a map with a peak called Machu Picchu.

1911

On July 24, Hiram Bingham III reaches Machu Picchu.

1913

National Geographic Magazine devotes its April 1913 issue to the 1912 Machu Picchu expedition.

1920

In October, Peru's diplomat to the United States asks for the artifacts' return.

1948

Bingham returns to Peru to help inaugurate the opening of a paved road to Machu Picchu.

1983

Machu Picchu is listed as a UNESCO World Heritage Site.

2000

The World Monument Fund includes Machu Picchu on its Watch List.

2008

In December, Peru sues Yale University to have all the Machu Picchu artifacts returned.

2012

On November 12, Yale returns the remaining artifacts to Peru.

DIGGING UP THE FACTS

DATE OF DISCOVERY

Hiram Bingham discovered Machu Picchu on July 24, 1911.

KEY PLAYERS

- Ellwood C. Erdis was an American engineer who joined Bingham's expedition.

- Hiram Bingham III was an American explorer who studied Machu Picchu.

- Pachacuti was the Inca leader who ordered the construction of Machu Picchu.

KEY TECHNOLOGIES

Cameras helped document the Machu Picchu site during early expeditions. Bone examination technology made it possible to identify the gender, occupation, and diet of the people buried at Machu Picchu.

IMPACT ON SCIENCE

Machu Picchu has helped archaeologists and scientists understand the Inca culture. The terraces, walls, and drainage system demonstrate advanced Inca engineering. Today, Machu Picchu stimulates discussion about the impact of tourism on historic sites.

GETTING THERE

November and April tend to be the least busy tourist months at Machu Picchu. The first step in traveling to the site is flying to Lima, Peru's capital. From there, travelers can take a bus or airplane to Cuzco. Then, they can take a train to a small city near the base of the mountain. From there, a bus takes visitors up steep, twisting roadways to the site. Alternately, people up to the challenge can take a two-hour hike up the path. Only a limited number of people per day are allowed into the site, so reserving a place far ahead of time is crucial.

QUOTE

"It seemed like an unbelievable dream. . . . It fairly took my breath away. What could this place be? Why had no one given us any idea of it?"—*Hiram Bingham*

GLOSSARY

antiquarian
A person who studies and collects antiques.

aqueduct
A structure for carrying a large quantity of flowing water.

archivist
A person in charge of historical documents or public records.

chalice
A drinking cup.

conquistador
Spanish conquerors of civilizations in South and Central America.

cranial
Relating to the skull.

curator
A person who is in charge of a museum or collection.

mausoleum
A large tomb.

muleteer
A person who drives mules.

niche
A boxlike shelf carved into a wall.

osteology
The study of bones.

potsherd
A pottery fragment.

reconnaissance
A preliminary survey to collect information.

topography
The art of drawing detailed maps of natural or manmade features of a location.

trepanation
The operation of boring holes in the skull to release pressure.

ADDITIONAL RESOURCES

SELECTED BIBLIOGRAPHY

Burger, Richard L., and Lucy C. Salazar. *Machu Picchu: Unveiling the Mystery of the Incas*. New Haven, CT: Yale U P, 2004. Print.

MacQuarrie, Kim. *The Last Days of the Incas*. New York: Simon, 2007. Print.

FURTHER READINGS

Gruber, Beth. *Ancient Inca: Archaeology Unlocks the Secrets of the Inca's Past*. Washington, DC: National Geographic, 2006. Print.

Lewin, Ted. *Lost City: The Discovery of Machu Picchu*. New York: Philomel, 2003. Print.

WEBSITES

To learn more about Digging Up the Past, visit **booklinks.abdopublishing.com**. These links are routinely monitored and updated to provide the most current information available.

FOR MORE INFORMATION

For more information on this subject, contact or visit the following organizations:

YALE PEABODY MUSEUM OF NATURAL HISTORY
Yale University
PO Box 208118
New Haven, CT 06520
203-432-5004
http://peabody.yale.edu
The anthropology collection at Yale's Peabody Museum features documents, photos, and artifacts from the Yale Peruvian Expedition.

YALE UNIVERSITY STERLING MEMORIAL LIBRARY
120 High Street
New Haven, CT 06511
203-432-1775
http://www.library.yale.edu/building/sterling-library
Yale's Sterling Memorial Library owns papers and photos from the Peruvian expeditions, as well as Bingham's personal papers.

SOURCE NOTES

Chapter 1. Mysterious Gem in the Sky

1. "Machu Picchu." *Encyclopaedia Britannica*. Encyclopaedia Britannica, 2014. Web. 7 Jan. 2014.

2. "One Million Tourists Visit Machu Picchu in 2011." *Peruvian Times*. Peruvian Times, 20 Nov. 2011. Web. 7 Jan. 2014.

3. "Notes." *Secret of the Incas*. Turner Classic Movies, 2014. Web. 7 Jan. 2014.

Chapter 2. Hide and Seek

1. Kim MacQuarrie. *Last Days of the Incas*. New York: Simon, 2007. Print. 45.

2. "Inca." *Encyclopaedia Britannica*. Encyclopaedia Britannica, 2014. Web. 7 Jan. 2014.

3. Kim MacQuarrie. *Last Days of the Incas*. New York: Simon, 2007. Print. 448.

4. Christopher Heaney. *Cradle of Gold: The Story of Hiram Bingham, a Real-Life Indiana Jones, and the Search for Machu Picchu*. New York: Palgrave, 2010. Print. 93.

5. Richard Burger and Lucy Salazar. *Machu Picchu: Unveiling the Mystery of the Incas*. New Haven, CT: Yale U P, 2004. Print. 66.

Chapter 3. Into the Clouds

1. Kim MacQuarrie. *Last Days of the Incas*. New York: Simon, 2007. Print. 393.

2. Hiram Bingham. *Lost City of the Incas*. London: Phoenix, 1952. Print. 178.

3. Roger Balm. "The Expeditionary Eye: Reconstructing the First Photographs of Machu Picchu, Peru." *Focus on Geography* 47.4 (2004): 9. Print.

4. Hiram Bingham. *Lost City of the Incas*. London: Phoenix, 1952. Print. 179.

5. Ibid.

6. Ibid.

7. Christopher Heaney. *Cradle of Gold: The Story of Hiram Bingham, a Real-Life Indiana Jones, and the Search for Machu Picchu*. New York: Palgrave, 2010. Print. 91.

8. Ibid. 127.

Chapter 4. Return to Peru

1. Christopher Heaney. *Cradle of Gold: The Story of Hiram Bingham, a Real-Life Indiana Jones, and the Search for Machu Picchu.* New York: Palgrave, 2010. Print. 130.

2. Ibid. 133.

3. Amy Cox Hall. "Collecting a 'Lost City' for Science: Huaquero Vision and the Yale Peruvian Expeditions to Machu Picchu, 1911, 1912 and 1914-15." *Ethnohistory* 59.2 (2012): 302. Print.

Chapter 5. Widening the Search

1. Christopher Heaney. *Cradle of Gold: The Story of Hiram Bingham, a Real-Life Indiana Jones, and the Search for Machu Picchu.* New York: Palgrave, 2010. Print. 136.

2. George F. Eaton. *The Collection of Osteological Material from Machu Picchu.* New Haven, CT: Tuttle, 1916. Print. 94.

3. Richard Burger and Lucy Salazar. *Machu Picchu: Unveiling the Mystery of the Incas.* New Haven, CT: Yale U P, 2004. Print. 88.

4. Ibid. 95.

Chapter 6. Engineering Marvels

1. Kenneth R. Wright & Afredo Valencia Zegarra. *Machu Picchu: A Civil Engineering Marvel.* Reston, VA: American Society of Civil Engineers Press. Print. 36.

2. Ibid. 38.

3. Julian Smith. "Machu Picchu's Stairway of Fountains." *Archaeology* 66.1 (2013): 49. Print.

4. Kenneth R. Wright & Afredo Valencia Zegarra. *Machu Picchu: A Civil Engineering Marvel.* Reston, VA: American Society of Civil Engineers Press. Print. 26.

5. Richard Burger and Lucy Salazar. *Machu Picchu: Unveiling the Mystery of the Incas.* New Haven, CT: Yale U P, 2004. Print. 127.

6. Kenneth R. Wright & Afredo Valencia Zegarra. *Machu Picchu: A Civil Engineering Marvel.* Reston, VA: American Society of Civil Engineers Press. Print. 68.

Chapter 7. Inca Antiquities

1. Christopher Heaney. *Cradle of Gold: The Story of Hiram Bingham, a Real-Life Indiana Jones, and the Search for Machu Picchu.* New York: Palgrave, 2010. Print. 148–149.

2. George F. Eaton. *The Collection of Osteological Material from Machu Picchu.* New Haven, CT: Tuttle, 1916. Print. 23–29.

3. Christopher Heaney. *Cradle of Gold: The Story of Hiram Bingham, a Real-Life Indiana Jones, and the Search for Machu Picchu.* New York: Palgrave, 2010. Print. 149.

4. Ibid. 145.

5. Ibid. 155.

Chapter 8. A New Expedition

1. Christopher Heaney. *Cradle of Gold: The Story of Hiram Bingham, a Real-Life Indiana Jones, and the Search for Machu Picchu.* New York: Palgrave, 2010. Print. 166.

2. Ibid. 169.

3. Ibid. 176.

4. Amy Cox Hall. "Collecting a 'Lost City' for Science: Huaquero Vision and the Yale Peruvian Expeditions to Machu Picchu, 1911, 1912 and 1914-15." *Ethnohistory* 59.2 (2012): 305. Print.

5. Christopher Heaney. *Cradle of Gold: The Story of Hiram Bingham, a Real-Life Indiana Jones, and the Search for Machu Picchu.* New York: Palgrave, 2010. Print. 186.

6. Ibid. 191.

Chapter 9. The Modern Machu Picchu

1. Richard Burger and Lucy Salazar. *Machu Picchu: Unveiling the Mystery of the Incas.* New Haven, CT: Yale U P, 2004. Print. 87.

2. "UNESCO Calls for 'Emergency Measures' to Protect Machu Picchu." *Global Heritage Fund.* Global Heritage Fund, 8 June 2012. Web. 7 Jan. 2014.

INDEX

ABOUT THE AUTHOR

Mary Meinking grew up in Iowa looking for arrowheads and dreaming of being an archaeologist. Instead she became a graphic designer and writer. Her nonfiction articles have been published in a dozen different children's magazines. Mary has written more than two dozen nonfiction books about arts and crafts, extreme jobs, animals, pop stars, and history. When not working, writing, or hanging out with her family, Mary enjoys doing arts and crafts, baking, gardening, and traveling.